A myriad of words

S Williams

BookLeaf Publishing

India | USA | UK

Presentation by *BookLeaf Publishing*

Web: www.bookleafpub.com

E-mail: info@bookleafpub.com

ISBN : 9789358361049

First edition 2021

1.

Eyes that crinkle

Skin with folds

Limber limbs and arms that hold.

Hair too long

Freckles dot the cheeks

A smile so big, the whitest teeth.

A heart of gold that beats so strong

Full of love and fire and song.

Belly, soft, that rolls with laughs

Fuels the body and takes you far.

A mind that's bright and full of ideas
questions that only you can hear.

The lightest soul carrying you through

keeping you on the straight and true.

Oh what a wonder it is to live to be a

small part in a world such a this.

A reminder to love what makes you you

through triumphs and troubles, great or

few.

2.

Words fall on deaf ears

Hearts become heavy with doubt

Eyes avoid and mouths silence

Love sees through the empty spaces

Beyond the weight that lingers

Rather miserable together because we'd

be miserable apart

3.

At the mere thought

Just a sparkle in my eye

My heart blooms.

A thousand petals flowing outward, at
the simple imagined version of you.

My womb feels full and complete as
though its purpose was only ever you.

I imagine your first breath and feel a
rush of fire and life.

As though my reason for breathing was
only ever to create you.

My blood courses in your veins a fire in
your heart lit by mine.

A small breath of my air to encourage
your flames to grow

What would I give if not everything for
you.

4.

Fluffy paws, the wettest chin

A waggy tail and toothy grin.

Your brown eyes look to us with great
expectation a day full of fun and walks -
your 'vacation'.

Though you may not be old, you have
seen such things a quiet spy in a house
of human beings.

Your companionship is really like no
other your loyalty, trust and friendship is
no bother.

Do not fear, wee pup, that if you are ill a
warm blanket and cuddles will help you
get well.

And if it is wet and we make you go

walkies a towel will be waiting to dry

your wee pawsies.

Every morning you greet us with a yawn

and a stretch, that wee waggy tail and

an expectation of fetch.

River walks, sea strolls and zoomies

through the house barks and snuffles

and searching for a mouse.

O' dirty paws and fluffy bearded beast,

we love you so, our companion, not

least.

5.

Sharper than a fresh knife

they slice

clean cuts or flesh wounds

they bleed

quick thoughts lead to fast words

which damage beyond repair

unable to forget

6.

A cool wind blows across my face

Eyes staring upwards

The dull sun hides behind greying
clouds

My back slightly dampened by the grass

Petrichor fills my senses as water drops
from the sky

I close my eyes and melt into the earth

7.

Softly on my skin

like a water droplet running up my arm

Eyes shielded

Brighter than light itself I glide.

Hearts soaring

Grass cool underfoot

Swallows soar

Our eyes meet

We become one.

8.

The building of pressure

The words The feelings

Bubbling, boiling, burning

Doubt fills my head

Head full of worry

The building of pressure

A breath

Kind words

Shoulders drop

A sigh

 Its okay to not be okay.

9.

You glow

Warmth radiates

Bright yellow and joyful

I shine in the dark orbiting you

My sun and your moon

I only shine because you glow.

10.

Doubt so strong it cripples my structure

crumbles to the floor

I stood on firm ground until the opinions

of others kicked my legs out from under

me

11.

Ever stretching dark

A star, the brightest of sparks

A light at the end of the tunnel

The sun always rises tomorrow.